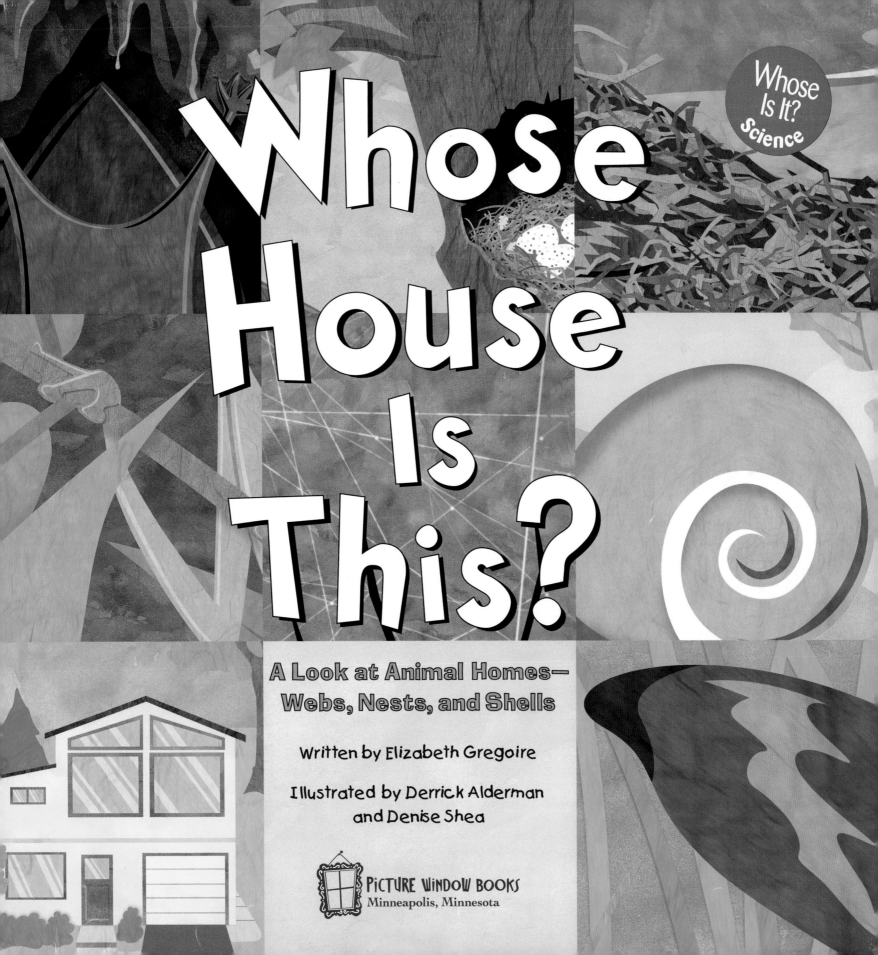

Whose House Is This?

Whose Is It? Science

A Look at Animal Homes—Webs, Nests, and Shells

Written by Elizabeth Gregoire

Illustrated by Derrick Alderman
and Denise Shea

PICTURE WINDOW BOOKS
Minneapolis, Minnesota

Special thanks to our advisers for their expertise:

Debbie Folkerts, Ph.D.
Assistant Professor of Biological Sciences
Auburn University, Alabama

Susan Kesselring, M.A., Literacy Educator
Rosemount-Apple Valley-Eagan (Minnesota) School District

Managing Editors: Bob Temple, Catherine Neitge
Creative Director: Terri Foley
Editors: Nadia Higgins, Patricia Stockland
Editorial Adviser: Andrea Cascardi
Storyboard Development: Amy Bailey Muehlenhardt
Designer: Nathan Gassman
Page production: Banta
The illustrations in this book were prepared digitally.

Picture Window Books
5115 Excelsior Boulevard
Suite 232
Minneapolis, MN 55416
877-845-8392
www.picturewindowbooks.com

Library of Congress Cataloging-in-Publication Data
Gregoire, Elizabeth.
Whose house is this? : a look at animal homes—webs, nests,
and shells / by Elizabeth Gregoire ; illustrated by Derrick
Alderman and Denise Shea.
p. cm. — (Whose is it?)
Includes bibliographical references and index.
ISBN 1-4048-0608-3 (reinforced lib. bdg.)
1. Animals—Habitations—Juvenile literature. I. Alderman,
Derrick, ill. II. Shea, Denise, ill. III. Title. IV. Series.

QL756.G65 2004
591.56'4—dc22   2004000863

Come on in, and find a clue about who's who.

Look closely at an animal's house. It can be a huge cave or a tiny leaf. An animal's house can be a soft nest or a hard shell. It can stretch across a dusty corner of your house.

A lot of animals use their houses to stay safe from hungry predators. A house can offer shade from the sun. It can be a place for storing food or taking a long winter nap.

Animals' houses don't all look alike because they don't all work alike.

Can you tell whose house is whose?

Look in the back for more fun facts about houses.

Whose house is this, dangling on a tree?

4

5

This is a red-eyed tree frog's leaf.

During the day, this frog may sleep under a leaf of a rain forest tree. The cool shade keeps the frog's skin moist. At night, the tiny frog leaps from leaf to leaf, searching for insects to eat.

Fun fact: A red-eyed tree frog has suction cups on the tips of its toes. That's why it can climb on skinny leaves and branches without falling off.

Whose house is this,
stretching from wall to wall?

This is a black widow spider's web.

Its house works like a trap. When a beetle wanders into the spider's web, it gets tangled up. The beetle becomes the spider's supper.

Not-so-fun fact: Watch out! A black widow spider might bite people when she is guarding eggs in her web.

8

Whose house is this, sliding so slowly on a garden path?

9

This is a snail's shell.

A snail carries its house on its back. When the snail gets scared, it pulls its soft body inside the hard shell. Hungry animals will find something easier to munch for lunch.

Fun fact: Land snails have to keep moist. If the weather gets too dry, the snail seals itself inside its shell. It makes a door out of dried slime.

Whose house is this, so soft and cozy?

11

This is an arctic hare's nest.

The arctic ground is hard. An arctic hare can't dig a burrow the way some other rabbits do. In spring, the mother makes a cozy nest from grass and her own fur instead.

Fun fact: In winter, the arctic hare is white. It blends in with the snowy ground. In spring, the hare turns color to blend in with its nest.

Whose house is this, poking out of a rushing river?

13

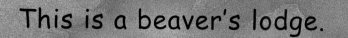

This is a beaver's lodge.

A beaver family lives here. The busy beavers built the lodge out of sticks and mud. The entrances to the lodge are under water. That keeps hungry predators from coming in.

Fun fact: A beaver family often builds a dam in front of the lodge. The dam blocks the river. The dam keeps the water around the lodge high enough to cover the entrances.

14

Whose house
is this,
high up in
a backyard tree?

15

This is a nuthatch's nest.

A nuthatch builds its
nest in a roomy hole
inside a tree.
The bird smears
crushed insects
around the opening.
The insect bodies
change the smell of the
nest. Predators won't know
there are eggs inside.

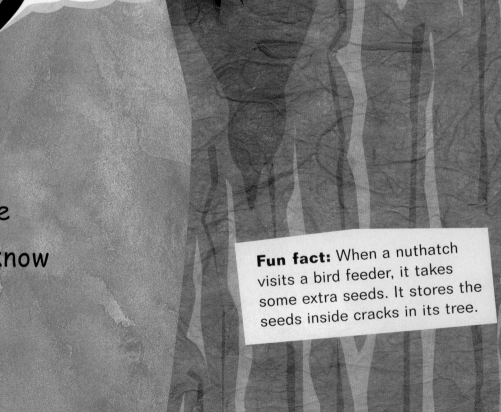

Fun fact: When a nuthatch
visits a bird feeder, it takes
some extra seeds. It stores the
seeds inside cracks in its tree.

Whose house is this, so dark and spooky?

This is a bat's cave.

In winter, a big group of bats hibernates in a cave. The bats sleep hanging upside down from the cave's ceiling. They huddle together to stay warm.

Fun fact: When it isn't hibernating, a bat stays in its house only during the day. It leaves at night to hunt.

Whose house is this,
in the middle of the block?

This is your house!

Like a bat, you sleep in your house. You live with your family, just like a beaver. Your house keeps you as cozy as an arctic hare and as safe as a snail. What else does your house do?

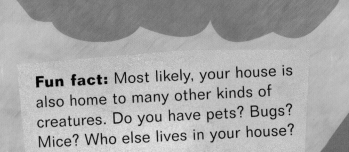

Fun fact: Most likely, your house is also home to many other kinds of creatures. Do you have pets? Bugs? Mice? Who else lives in your house?

Just for Fun

Make a coin bank house. (Get an adult to help you.)

What you need:

- cardboard milk carton (any size)

- glue

- scissors

- colored paper

- crayons, markers, or colored pencils

- cloth scraps and other decorations

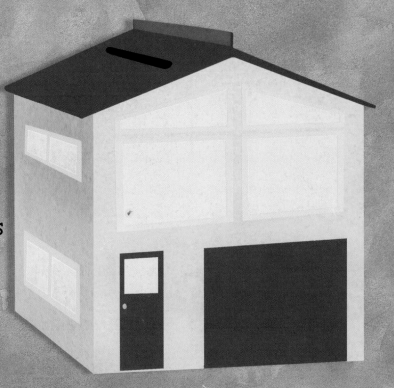

What you do:

1. Carefully open the milk carton at the top. Clean and dry the inside. Close up the carton again, and glue it shut.

2. Cut four pieces of colored paper to cover the four sides of the milk carton. Glue the paper on the carton.

3. Decorate the milk carton to make it look like your own house. Draw windows and doors. Glue cloth on the top to make a roof.

4. Have an adult cut a slot at the top of the milk carton. Whenever you have some extra coins, drop them in the slot.

Fun Facts About Animal Houses

Honey House
As many as 60,000 honeybees live together in a hive. All the bees in the hive have the same mother—the queen bee. The bees make the hive out of wax from their bodies. They use the hive for storing honey and raising young.

A Huge Nest
An eagle's nest is called an aerie. (Aerie sounds like "airy.") Eagles use the same aeries year after year. Each time they use the nests, the eagles make them a little bigger. An old aerie could be 10 feet (3 meters) wide and 15 feet (4½ meters) deep. You and several of your friends could easily fit inside a nest that size!

Home Sweet Home
A female green sea turtle will swim thousands of miles across open sea to return to the beach where she was born. She digs a hole in the sand and lays her eggs. She makes her nest in almost the exact same spot where she was hatched.

Icy Houses
Walruses live in freezing-cold oceans. In winter, they sometimes rest on big chunks of floating ice called floes. A walrus uses its long front teeth like hooks to pull its huge body onto the floe.

A Good Place to Hide
A prairie dog is a rodent that makes a sound like a barking dog. It lives in a deep, underground burrow. A prairie dog leaves piles of dirt around the entrances to the burrow. It hides behind the piles while it looks out for predators.

Words to Know

burrow—a kind of animal home such as a tunnel or hole in the ground

dam—a wall that stretches across a river; it slows down the rushing water and raises the water level behind it

hibernate—when an animal spends the whole winter in a kind of deep sleep; animals hibernate to save energy when the weather is cold and there isn't much food to eat

moist—things that are just a little wet

predator—an animal that hunts and eats other animals

To Learn More

At the Library

Dahl, Michael. *Do Parrots Have Pillows? A Book About Where Animals Sleep.* Minneapolis: Picture Window Books, 2003.

Shields, Carol Diggory. *Homes.* Brooklyn, N.Y.: Handprint Books, 2001.

Taylor, Barbara. *Animal Hide and Seek.* New York: Dorling Kindersley Publishing, 1998.

On the Web

FactHound offers a safe, fun way to find Web sites related to this book. All of the sites on FactHound have been researched by our staff. *www.facthound.com*

1. Visit the FactHound home page.
2. Enter a search word related to this book, or type in this special code: 1404806083.
3. Click the FETCH IT button.

Your trusty FactHound will fetch the best Web sites for you!

Index

Look for all the books in this series:

Whose Ears Are These?
A Look at Animal Ears—Short, Flat, and Floppy

Whose Eyes Are These?
A Look at Animal Eyes—Big, Round, and Narrow

Whose Feet Are These?
A Look at Hooves, Paws, and Claws

Whose Food Is This?
A Look at What Animals Eat—Leaves, Bugs, and Nuts

Whose House Is This?
A Look at Animal Homes—Webs, Nests, and Shells

Whose Legs Are These?
A Look at Animal Legs—Kicking, Running, and Hopping

Whose Mouth Is This?
A Look at Bills, Suckers, and Tubes

Whose Nose Is This?
A Look at Beaks, Snouts, and Trunks

Whose Shadow Is This?
A Look at Animal Shapes—Round, Long, and Pointy

Whose Skin Is This?
A Look at Animal Skin—Scaly, Furry, and Prickly

Whose Sound Is This?
A Look at Animal Noises—Chirps, Clicks, and Hoots

Whose Spots Are These?
A Look at Animal Markings—Round, Bright, and Big

Whose Tail Is This?
A Look at Tails—Swishing, Wiggling, and Rattling

Whose Work Is This?
A Look at the Things Animals Make—Pearls, Milk, and Honey